DRIVE THROUGH THE
BLUE CYLINDERS

Also by Ed Friedman

The New Space (1973)
The Black Star Pilgrimage (1977)
The New York Hat Line (with Robert Kushner and Katherine
    Landman, 1979)
The Telephone Book (1979)
La Frontera (with Kim MacConnel, 1983)
Humans Work (1988)
Mao & Matisse (1995)
Away (with Robert Kushner, 2001)
The Funeral Journal (2001)

DRIVE THROUGH THE BLUE CYLINDERS

Ed Friedman

Hanging Loose Press
Brooklyn, New York

Thanks to the editors of publications in which many of these works first appeared: *Arshile, Bathos, Blade, canwehaveourballback, Conjunctions, Food & Water Journal, Hanging Loose, Insurance, Pagan Place, The Portable Boog Reader, Shiny,* and *The World.*

Thanks to the many friends who read early versions of "Away" and made helpful suggestions.

Hanging Loose Press thanks the Literature Program of the New York State Council on the Arts and the Fund for Poetry for grants in support of the publication of this book.

Printed in the United States of America
10 9 8 7 6 5 4 3 2 1

Cover art and author photo by Lori Landes
Additional cover design by Pamela Flint

          Library of Congress Cataloging-in-Publication Data
Friedman, Ed
    Driving through the blue cylinders / Ed Friedman
        p. cm.
    ISBN 1-882413-96-2 -- ISBN 1-882413-95-4 (pbk.)
    I. Title.

PS3556.R5186 D7 2001
811'.54--dc21   00-050038

Produced at The Print Center, Inc., 225 Varick St., New York, NY 10014, a non-profit facility for literary and arts-related publications. (212) 206-8465

for Lori and Sam

Contents

DRIVE THROUGH THE BLUE CYLINDERS

Position

Elevators whiz
We move moth-like
Causing pictures in each other
To shine waters
You can leave anytime
A palmful of grass
And fall for a great city
Coolness fills
The dreamy
Veer between taxis
Polarizing stretches
Of sunwarmed lawn
Orange tree shadows
Shape every luster
Ample and searing
My wife's love
Without our having met
Would be electricity
In violet grasses
Creeping over a busy life
Being breezy
Trout fishermen
With brushed red hair
Breathe as we do
When nothing special happens
At the other end of the line
Is me and some white print
Billowing leisurely
Secret codes
Myriad evanescent faint

It's four a.m.
In the world of a bat
Daydreaming a lake
After wind disturbance
Swings in
Flicks around
Tree-frog voices
Every time our fantastic eyebrows
Curve and spread
Incessant force
Drives waves of change
I get up I sit down
I get up again
As an insect I'd barely be
A flutter in warm silence
But you like me
Much more than that so
I have expanse
Leaves stem
Legs float away
A leech falls down
Through morning clouds
Blue banners
Pressure and stillness
Are ideas of danger
Doughnut-size
They play along
Sensual, eager
Flowing furiously by
Whenever I see mist or
Mistake you for an acquaintance

Life feels long
All potted palms
Dispersing amiably
Eight stories down to
Sway harbor waters
On pebbled glass
Never until now
Equals always even then
We ease palely through
Each instant traced as network
Cut from filmy moves
A float of the hand
Stealth isn't something new
A tall cool plenty
For a nice long cosy
Row house lights
Send shadows down sleepless
Under fine thick gray ice
Loon-like
Milkmen go home
Spread helplessly
You get pretty damn touchy
Not breathing
A minute or two
The road authentic
Sky pops out of itself
No more secret
Than fresh motions
Smudge depths to liquify
Morning and confidence
In simple tomato patterns

To view land and never leave
Means rule
Fuss with details
Propped up in history
Make incalculable progress
We feel good about
Appliance-switch clicks
Table-lamp glows
Enabling definite kinds
Down waxed car paint gleam
Eighty warrior clams
Seclude themselves swaying
Lipstick smears
Fleurs-de-bain powders
Ripple oceany
Pink basins
Barley waves
Bulges and so on
Swish among differences
Labor serious not hard
You look like your photo
A comfort come to me
Entire afternoons
Thrill with long slanting
Impressionable skies
The bus rolls on
The pond snails salute
Put your hips against mine
And invade the simple
With cricket voices
Tall dark torchy you

4

Bend your face to where
Shine whirls pass on
That random faithfulness
You make a friend
Fit between
And drawn slowly in
Half an hour later
We're aware of rushing
Very beautiful pictures
My mountain village
Earthen tiles wall
The shape of Los Angeles
With grasses so deep
We nod about
Playful and eager
Unsure time passes
Ornamental, purplish
Audible at moments
Saying now and now again
You seem as they say
Dyed in sorrow
Much of you soft
Riding on wind
The work as I see it
Looms through the present
Memory and perception
The ways cold warms up
Fingers to your lips
Insert a cherry lifesaver
You never forget
This kindness that grace

Melt away
Currents of purpose
Tough to get along with
When nothing outside them
Signals revelation
Look at the moon
's special message
To no one thing
All is part rising
Deer under it
Approach cold flecks of light
Green as fluorescent
Wristwatch numbers in the dark
Is a drive-in movie
Miles away
Many in cars are watching
My hero
The one I wait for
With pumpkin dinner
Smoking I mean
Steaming on the table
Pleasant pastel shades
Formally acquire resemblance to food
From my open-hearted gesture
"Here. I made it just for you!"
Delicate, filtered, sharpened
We say enough and mean
I need much more
To really live as myself
Resting wave upon wave
Singing flying singing

The limits of time
Whatever your intentions
Are unrequited
For as little as all
The inches you travel
Dream a whole life
And come upon it
Lantern held up
Leaning so far forward
As not to need more steps
Only to end up
Go further on

AWAY

Calling All Cars

There's a monumental snowman behind us, we salute, and winter's black sky fills with bright stars. Where is Mom? Could she be diving in the Olympics again, with Dad or some muscular passerby waving to her from poolside? We know that modern art is representative of something called "mind" or "experience," but walking along with burning questions such as these is never soothing. I know, through stems and leaves we'll make our way by the pond towards home! There's a not-yet-open smell to air. Moonlight shines white on hands that point towards where home might be. Slender, uncertain, shadowed, you have always been dear to me like mourning doves or moored speedboats on distant Lake Michigan. All the elbowing-each-other-out-of-the-way we've done to get a glimpse of anything precious has been long since forgiven. We set out.

Verge

By a soft approach through paved alleys we carry fresh water in blue-gray canteens and admire the calm shallows of La Jolla Cove. We've had many arguments by now but my favorite is one about a sea bass dancing near an old shard that has a female nude painted on it. You claim that the only significance of this occurrence is one we contrive. I am adamant that the fish is experiencing sexual attraction to the woman, and that she is ravenous for seafood. Don't you think we've done a lot of bending today? My hips need stroking or to be settled firmly on mossy ground.

Free Market

"Whir, toot, and drone" describes the melody of a shawm-blowing fakir who sits cross-legged in the marketplace. Minarets partition the fine purplish blue tweediness of utterly perfect desert sky. "We couldn't have stayed at home and known this," you say.

"Not in such vibrant detail," I say.

It's having the general siphoned off from the specific, or venetian blinds open on a glimpse of wishing. A life that nobody has to answer for—that's what we're after. Sunset and sunrise on the lower edge of remembering. Our eyes, round as archery targets, subsume the unfolding vista.

Slipping In

Imagine we enter your land waving our banner of truth over the earth's dry surface. We're prepared to analyze every molecule magnified to the size of a pea. You stretch out like rubber and advance past us in giant teaspoons. This isn't right, so we'll arrive less presumptuously, in a late-model car with bumper stickers proclaiming that we've been to Atlantic City. Why do birds here have miniaturized dimensions? Do young cedars planted at the base of fertile hills hold sway over otherwise arid landscape? And what will you know of us? Of us!

Moisten, Dry

Meanwhile we collect postcards. A camel in the late afternoon sun looks over its left shoulder towards the Pyramids of Gizeh. Then we're underwater with spotted eel for some solid moments of floating this way and that. Swans above us on moonlit rivers are ours for as long as we visualize them. When we get home and apply our new-found imagination to the rigors of every day, it will be no trouble to replace lightbulbs and governments, housing tracts and vegetable gardens. Once Sheila the Moth landed on a bamboo stalk to peer at the night sky and stayed there until she was a dried husk. Books fill with stories like these. Aquariums house the lives of swooping angelfish.

Overlook

These are some really big trees. The trunks are the width of a person, no, *two* persons. The waviness in the sky is about perfect. Isn't it worth climbing impossible rock escarpments to arrive at such wonders? What efforts of this sort might I make on you? Are there hidden cities in your personality? An arched trellis of golden orange roses stretches between my desire for homecoming and your pursuit of consensual truth.

After Them

What occupies me most is posture: the triangulation of the North Star relative to a corporate office building and my confident upright gaze. Our arms are by our sides, and we are strutting. The clean-shaven guide points with vigor to a glow which he says originates in an invisible ocean. Travel is force. It's expenditure and accrual. Mom, as a young woman, worked several jobs to make this all possible, as did Father who was also a staunch nurturer. And their parents before them. With you now, I am your correspondent and confidant. I stroke each letter onto the page as if it were an unending life. My spine is as straight as a lower-case "l" and my mouth is a perfect "O" of gaping surprise.

Making Tracks

Look at our big harvest dresses and babushkas. As is customary, we stroll among local farmers through the rank wheat fields. We carry tablets with heroic phrases inscribed on them. "Full throttle!" "Bare-assed fast!" "Replete pantries!" One of the ambitious young peasants, mallet and chisel in hand, is engraving agricultural narratives on the granite capitols of a homestead. Her brother is lying on the lawn reading about the breath of buffaloes and their drinking habits near major waterways. Everything today feels historic. Don't the clouds and birds look like writing in the sky?

Singularity Among Equals

Someone who wants to go beyond what anyone else thinks even to find out for him- or herself what everyone else already knows leaves home for a life that won't seem daily or routine for awhile. I'm now sleeping much of the day and waking up in the late afternoon to paint your picture in the hours of magical light. Summer evenings are bright until long after dinner, and though no one recommends gardening at this hour, I'm out in rolling green fields under quiet calm blue sky. Sometimes on the road I'll see an eccentric person in the garb of a culture no one's ever heard of. She will be humming intelligently and gliding along as if dance were her only means of locomotion.

Dippers

When I swan-dive over the bay, waters beneath me appear blue and soft or hard and dangerous, but for whole moments I am captivated by flight. The supple arch in my back. The breeze through my armpits. I am aloft, and from surrounding hillsides or tacking sailboats everyone can see me so. I have peered down darkened corridors and this is nothing like that. I've come crashing to the turf trying to get my hands on an elusive fumbled football and this is nothing like that either. I watch you dive, observing the perfect extension of your feet towards the heavens around you. Joining me in the tropical waters, you surface with that "glad look." Will there be a permanent ripple in our bellies from when we tilted over the cliff's edge towards free-fall? No? Then let's do it again.

Known Figments

We make a point of sightseeing while the city sleeps. At early dawn or late Sunday afternoon, streets, docks, and construction sites are virtually empty. I know our minds well enough to watch them shift in these deserted locales and what it is in us that craves seeing things when they aren't in use. We'd like to drive that dump truck through the new Theban temple and rearrange colorful signal flags strung fore to aft on an anchored oil barge. Telephone wires suspended on wooden poles above a Himalayan suburb await messages of unknown quality and kinds. Light in the water. Light from the skies. Gleams on the rails of the railway lines.

Ductile

Look at the out-of-scale world we're in. I can stand in a well-tailored raincoat and fedora staring at a traffic accident while smoke from your cigar envelopes the whole scene. I was thinking of my tea set once and my head shrank to the size of a small kettle. What is the appropriate music for such pliable circumstances? Could it be small-combo jazz? Faint whistling performed by a retiree in her reclining easy chair? As no one may ever have this same knowledge again we must envision what we want and then seek it. Ambitious, serene, dedicated, and flighty we persist in raising expectations even in times that foment diminishment.

Guided and Free

When Daddy carried me on his back through fig groves, he told me about being a dancer with voluminous petticoats. "All the men," he said, "believed that the dances and petticoats were for them." I could have been a movie star, a studio mogul, or the king-face on a deck of playing cards, but to myself I was always moving with my arms around his neck, hearing him talk to me as if I were of the past and future. Imagine me in clean denim traveling towards home. Poplars swayed in the wind. Wrens hid among the branches. We could troll in a bark canoe for lake trout and all the while have a Thermos of hot soup awaiting us for lunch. Such coming and going has familial warmth in which rates of exchange are fascinating concerns as are echelons of pictures set into others or standing free. Perhaps when I say "pictures," you will understand me to mean "moments" or "experiences," the way my father would.

Far and Wide

This land is dark and full of weather. In the week we've been here, many bird flocks have flown over without landing. I have read all the Greek classics in the Harvard collection of ancient poetry. They were in translation, of course, so I'll never know what any of them really mean. Mostly it was hubbub among men whose haircuts I can't imagine.

In the old days, Mom carried me in her arms. I would point, and she'd utter sounds which I came to know as "names." It was the beginning of a reading list: pig, furnace, bird cage, cloud, hula, etc. How long would she hold me? How far could we go and still have new words to say? Once while she was pregnant with my brother, we stood under telephone lines in the wind. I wasn't wondering about my father, but a feeling was building inside me that someone dear was missing. No movement or distraction could defer the growing prominence of this mood.

Transponder

Start at position A, the beautiful but treacherous inland waterway. With multiple communications media—phone, pen, and radio waves— we proliferate our travel. Minds and imaginations follow our every maneuver. We take off through puffy cloud cover and scatter airmail envelopes over an immense industrial park. Now, we're floating downstream on a decorative barge. Wailing babies and horse whinnies! Our world is full of unintelligible utterance. My assignment has been to recognize distances. Now I do. For you, it's been a matter of too much trouble regulating temperature shifts, but at last you assume a complete adaptability. Mom and Dad will be pleased that we've continued our mission, even if they have no idea why. Together we live on in their absence, but our memories of them remain fixed. Travel the memory. Propel it through uncharted miles. Can the parents we hold in mind evolve without their being here?

Late Entry

The first question we have, when entering a new territory, is whether or not the striped road leading to a picturesque stone outcropping permits romantic interludes along the way. The specter of a man from our collective past looms over a revolver and a school teacher. Intrigue or sporting event? Acting as if we're entirely welcome, we stroll through the center of town in rugby uniforms. I have the number "1" embroidered on the front of my shirt, and you have "2." I am waving as if people have nothing better to do than applaud my presence. You rapidly note all response, which turns out to be minimal, since most of the locals are sitting outdoors in stuffed hotel-lobby chairs, with seemingly a lot on their minds. There is no conversation. No cheering. In fact, it's nap time only everyone's awake.

"We've really got to get out of here," I say. "I've seen this before. It's like being babies among adults. We have so much to live for and they seemingly have so little. Eventually they will want what we have until we don't have it anymore."

You say, "Wrong. This is a good land with a blithe and unassuming populace. You're wearing a jockstrap that's two sizes too small and you expect everyone's sympathy because your nuts are being squeezed. The people probably think you like it this way, and they're probably right!"

Inner Mongolia

When a construction crane hoists air-conditioning units over a fuel refinery, you can be distracted by a radiant inner city. Across groomed lawns in the direction of sunset is perfectly proportioned skyline. Precious-metal-leafed domes top every rectangular solid. From every dome, a proud needle extends skyward. The industrial waterfront behind us is the source of an informational radioactivity. Disbursed particles of know-how interact unpredictably with thought. Let's intrude randomly on minds at work.

"I've told you many times that I prefer junks to luxury ocean liners, but here we are, steaming past Hawaii on the Queen Elizabeth, surrounded by shuffleboard aficionados who think they can work off eight meals a day by shoving a rubber doohickey around with oversized spatulas."

"It's the stilt city we're after—a dangerous idea with a base equal to the area of Brazil. We exist among these concepts and experiments. When the waters threaten our fragile outpost, natives have a few choice sarcasms to utter."

"As travel companions we're everything anyone could ever desire. It's as citizens, I'm afraid, we're a bust."

"This is why there must exist within atoms very great forces of attraction to hold us together. Otherwise, darling, we would explode."

Dairy Yen

As thoughts flow between us in frames on a 70 mm strip of Technicolor movie celluloid, we are rounding up our newly acquired cow herd. How to milk these massive black and white mammals is a matter for research. We can see in each others' minds image after image of ourselves reading and being read to: alone; with mother; in smoky dormitory rooms, etc. Pages filled with farm knowledge flicker by. In most instances when people read to us, our relationships with them mediate the text, but facts are still there to be had.

My fingers squeezing goat teats at the San Diego Zoo is the most relevant cross-reference we come up with, but I realize it's only an old dream fragment and nothing like a direct, waking experience. We also discover a vision of your brother's childhood friend being electrocuted when he tried to use an automatic milking machine to masturbate. Ugh! This animal husbandry is getting to be a complicated project.

Still, I've heard over and over again that having tamed farm animals increases our capacity for survival, and if worse comes to worse, I am willing to put my mouth around one of those massive udders and start sucking. My stomach involuntarily retches a little at the anticipated funkiness of getting so close to a dairy cow's underside. It's all motherhood and food, though, and this thought reassures me.

Rousing Vignettes

Everyone loves our effervescent correspondence. Stamps from a distant hemisphere thrill even the most casual postcard enthusiast. Who would believe pictures on these stamps are scenes from our memories? Wild horses fleeing a cyclone of immense proportions are our long lost friends. Those two swans gliding past a gravel pit craved any love and attention we had to offer. So many signs construed as impersonal public insignias originate in a mind over matter—like our intentions for a better world. You can take them for passing sentiments or as mandates for protracted engagement. Recently, we've been stewing over a letter you sent us carrying the insignia of a molting dodo. Are we being overly touchy?

Fan Out

"Let's dedicate our day to photographing a man lifting a dumbbell over his head. No, let's walk around in samurai costumes and kick up dust." This is what I'm thinking as I practice cello in our hotel room. Fingers on my left hand press and vibrate, issuing beauty through the air. You have another idea about today. It has something to do with curtains. I know that a dreamy satisfied look comes over your face whenever you are framed by billowy window treatments. You're also thinking that seven of us could occupy a row at the local nature cinema. Across the alley silhouettes of a man and woman are dancing on closed paper shutters. I could say that I am accompanying them—the couple—with my cello, but really I'm just watching their shadows.

Infinite Thrust

The constant changing attraction of the world brings me to my knees
in a Dutch cornfield. I've strode through dark whorls of peacock
feathers and shooting stars, and I have never been clearer than I am at
this moment about truth and permeable bodies. A water polo team
speeds along country highway to an Olympic pool with a million
instances in mind of wrongful dunkings. Intelligence is too unpre-
dictable for perpetual motion. We counterpoise stillness with
expression on all sides. Today. An Innocent. Cold breeze. I sing with
exceptional velocity.

Blastoff

Hair, feathers and wild dancing. Today we'll portray life at its natural celerity—standing in a ticket-buyers line for the movies. A curious scene surrounds us. I'm not even talking about the terrariums and jumping bean displays. No, we are here assembled shoulder to shoulder in a millionth of a second. The styles of grooming are incredibly various. Cultured behaviors even more so. It's a land of similarity and difference, peopled by multitudes anticipating the light beams of a movie projector. To my left is Thailand and to our right is a man drooling tobacco juice on his tie. "Mister, you're a maniac. If Dad were here he'd be calming you down." Landscapes carved into lacquer room-screens provide the equivalent to magnetic fields in thought. I'm thinking, I'm thinking. Words attain speeds approaching a billion miles an hour.

Power Glide

Energy is produced or harnessed. Otherwise it's impossible to go from modern world to modern world. Out the porthole of our 1957 Ford Thunderbird there is nature. Quiet snowy road with tire tracks leads off into darkened bush. You were telling me about a new form-fitting rayon dress when overhead flew the Presidential Jet containing our propelled little President. He has a mission that might be as important as ours—though, certainly not to us. We find ourselves wishing everyone well in their pursuits, knowing that our collective force is boundless. Buildings grow high, forests deep. Refineries blur in their purified steam.

Big Schlep

When it comes to hauling a load, you think you'd want a horse, but if you found a big enough beetle, you could really make some headway. You know, I'm tired of eating off the floor. The coffeepot looks great down here and everything, but couldn't we visit some countries that have tables? Pacify me. Dress me different. Everywhere we go I feel like I'm preceded by my hairy back and knobby elbows, even while I'm walking forward! When do we get to the land that considers these features attractive? When will the strength of edible snails be recognized as heroic? Formed and decomposed over the course of a day, a whole lifetime would be enough to load 100 20-ton railway cars transformed 2,400 times each second averaging the sublimity of unutilized reasons. Now the legs and thighs. What else points pertly upwards?

Cultivation

It is best to enter the political life of a nation with a suntan. Whether you lounge for hours on a public beach or borrow an ultraviolet lightbulb from the local dermatologist scarcely matters. You want to give the impression of being ripe and mature rather than someone who can be formed by prevailing conditions. Having traveled the westernmost side-valleys of the Rio Rimac and the paved highways leading to the Peruvian world's Andean roof, our complexions require no special seasoning.

Quite naturally we gravitate towards the local parade route. Environmental action groups march in well-choreographed formations. Clerks for an Unbridled Future, equipped with 6-foot-long well-sharpened pencils, jab at the air with their marking tools for emphasis. Their chants celebrate the powers of both lead and eraser in rewriting history. We make it a policy to pay rapt attention but not to cheer for any of the parading enclaves. As the day wears on, our silence begins to irritate other onlookers.

Customs House

Someone has pasted a sign on the seat of a young worker that says "my ass is a hospital, drive your ambulance in here." Unfamiliar with local customs, what should our response be? Let's kneel down and examine the situation from the vantage of an ancient foot servant or rise up very high on our toes and imagine ourselves behind the wheel of an ambulance filled with emergency war victims. Anyway you stack it, the dilemma originates in dubious sources of cultural wisdom, while the world as we scrutinize it turns. A game of players who hop about in flowing robes using spears for balance has been replaced by baseball, horseshoes, and grab-the-wet-meat. Tea is delivered. Poem-papers are strewn about the cabana. Later we will stand on a street corner only to have the city loom around us. Where has the sun gone and the moon's many phases?

Brochure

Write it down. Now take its picture. Carry the casserole on your head,
then admire... Oh hello! This is the palace of vertical hanging beads.
Three warriors invented it with cyclones and trophies, and in a minute
we'll have ten good reasons for having trekked here. Meanwhile, let's
record our impressions of the locals' crossbow practice. They don't
use targets but fire arrows directly into each others' extremities.
Sword-thrusting is rehearsed to the same effect. What a brave or
stupid nation we've stumbled into! We must not understand what
we're seeing. Eventually we'll discover that *healing and recovery* are
being tested, and that the small recreational craft drifting offshore are
miniature hospital ships wherein most of the populace recuperates
and resides.

Topography

You must know by now that the family who carries a slate monolith to the highest peak in the Andes wins a free vacation on the Black Sea. It's a twenty-year competition that even school children can enter as long as they intend to have families. Solomina, the enchanting swing band singer, has already stated her intention to quit the music business in time to find a stone tablet and have triplets, since if two families reach the same summit height, it will be the greater number of offspring that determines the victor. Everywhere on the streets men with bouquets serenade women in windows. Their songs allude to "the highest peak" and how these women will be taken there. Some of the more cynical courted ladies answer these pleas with the traditional folk tune "Why Don't You Just Take Me On Vacation You Cheapskate!" "Glub glub glub" is the sound of the traditional folk song being sung underwater.

Phone Ahead

Look at this: I'm dressed in gossamer Bedouin sheik robes and you're in a curve-flattering sleeveless cocktail dress. We are two minds in the same place with seething, consequential, yet mutually harmless views. Let's start with the Earth, and make a telephone call around it. Lift the receiver and exclaim "Hello, France?" See if anyone will connect you in such an indiscriminate way. Imagine it's a carefree enough world that someone will answer your call and conduct a perfectly charming conversation.

"How's the general strike over there? Seen any Nazis?"

"Why no, we're having a jolly afternoon on horseback. You should really try calling Afghanistan sometime—that plateau where instead of using a ball, they play polo with a dead cat."

If society suddenly rocketed into space, crashed on a new planet and then resumed its journey, a revolutionary temperament might take hold. Meanwhile we try to effect all this dynamism in place. I lick the wall. You solemnly read a newspaper. Will signs transform us through stories that unfold as we speak?

Sustained Truth

Everywhere we go ideas about how to make things better abound. For this very reason, I recommend making suggestion boxes and leaving them at every conceivable location. A shoe box with a slit in the top. An unused ceramic punch bowl (We say "ceramic" because crystal doesn't guarantee enough privacy.). Or you can even use an old brown paper lunch bag with its top rolled down—putting a medium-size rock in the bottom of this ingenious construction gives it stability.

The potency of anonymous suggestion is astounding. A nameless flying swords-woman in Mysore made an impassioned plea to end open-air trash burning, bringing clear skies to that holiest of cities for the first time in centuries. A forlorn muscle-man in Crete was able to gather everyone in his native village for some much-needed morning exercise routines.

An additional benefit of installing suggestion boxes is that we too, as helpful travelers, can convey our invaluable fresh impressions to problem-beleaguered residents. It's a romantic moment for us when we leave our suggestions. We are suffused with love and a sense of empowered well-being. Afterwards, we can only guess at all the good we've done.

Partial Proof

It was 28° F when we kissed by the limy butte. Later we paraded through town as No. 1 and No. 2, members of a world-champion athletic team. To sum up our experience, the immense star-of-Bethlehem-shaped ice crystals and sinewy cloud wisps moonlit in otherwise clear sky have made us delusional. We fret. We play snooker. We agonize over the role a loaded revolver will have in our encounter with the enshadowed bureaucrat. We know that totality exists somewhere, but there is no way to just stumble across it. The president of the republic is elected by the people and is supposed to represent the general attitude of the majority. I have portrayed this disposition in the oil painting *Our Advance*. Whispery yellows under frosted glass with purples, blues and greens run together in a sea of deep compression.

Protocol

When two catfish meet or waterbugs sleep, three hens peck and a lone thoroughbred rears at the rising sun. Demonstrators emerge from a morning fog bank. This is traveling everyone understands—arise with the workers and march. Since humans protest everywhere these days, parades merge and disperse, gradually leading us around the globe. We assimilate local slogans and the good will of masses everywhere. So far we've crossed Europe and are headed for Asia. Local crops and livestock vary a great deal, but the determination of the people is constant. We've entered a continuum of revolutionary alliance with high spirits and good food. Look at all this healthy thriving. Even our shoes last longer than usual.

Alacrity

That it's an active day in the universe goes without saying. Liberation armies surround St. Louis, and you'd swear bucking broncos had taken over the town. Every spot on Earth—must I say it?—is "the hot spot." You stand stiffly at your desk in an Elsa Schapparelli day-suit and nurse a bottle of homeopathic cough medicine, or you conduct the sweetest little regional orchestra that ever rehearsed in a sports arena. Everyone has their say. The most deft cosmic archers let fly with "directionless release." Somebody who isn't satisfied with anyone else's ideas will investigate a circle to find it round in a completely new way.

Egress

To enter the world of animals, we stop eating them. A hundred women squat and spread piles of dried corn around the plaza. Along every trail men file into town carrying children on their shoulders. We've had our last bipedal gallop in the highlands, I'm afraid, because once we're "with the creatures" we'll be romping through sky on four legs. Much in the way of motion will be instinctual. We smell oncoming rain. A fish walks by, smoking the pipe in its toothy lips. It's Uncle Herb! More himself than ever! Is it possible that so many people can find happiness as parrots and quail? Look at us! We're about to have sex as llamas—and it's true love.

Squirt

We meet as the spirits of a pineapple and an empty Coca-Cola bottle in the land of menacing betel palms. We've seen abandoned teacups left steaming on ironing boards and inverted sombreros with lightning bolts striking in them. I say, "Isn't there something you want to tell me about 'the statuesque?'"

"I was waiting for the world to be a different place," you say, "and now it is. We have come together to be the first bottle of fresh pineapple juice. Fill me oh plump thorny-skinned one with your glorious yellow liquid."

Igneous

Shortly after daybreak, the antelope stag dance appears on the horizon. So rapid and joyful are the movements of the local population, that they appear as volcanic eruptions against cloudy dawn skies. When you learn what people think in times like these, you understand why rituals are entirely worthwhile. Ancient stories hinder escape to an inconsequential present. A constant washing in and swishing out of intimate emotions accompanies every conversation. Above the wind's roar, I know you better now than I did my own sister. I refuse to believe that a giant hermaphroditic rooster laid this world; still, we can all be friends.

Marvel Comics

Through a powerful electron microscope we see a seal balancing an inflated model of Earth on its nose. Automatic scissors slice the gold foil backdrop, while only a blink away on a checkered table cloth there's a cup of hot cocoa whose fragrant steam rises ten feet towards a vaulted breakfast-room ceiling. We record our observations and put another specimen slide under this potent magnifier. Each vision or speck of universe is compelling for as long as we can elaborate on its implications. When we get to the houseplant being showered by mysterious black droplets, the window screen mesh turns new blossoms into glowing white loops.

Conveyor

Drive through the blue cylinders, and you'll see a movie projected on an immense tortoise-shell comb whose teeth are secured in the side of a monumental red Bartlett pear. "The right size" comes to mind because a fisherman empties his dump truck load of yesterday's catch in your parking space. Can you rise above a bad odor? Are you "big enough?" Fortunately, the movie is full of ideas about transport. Swedish jet liners. Military troop carriers. An old bedsheet firmly attached to your shoulders streams out behind you. You sing "Here I come to pave the way!" Whoosh! You're flying towards rescue and salvage operations that have been awaiting a heroine for decades.

Pagoda Power

An eyebrow arched in surprise can be a whole continent if you look at it long enough. You smoke menthol cigarettes. I perform *tai chi* in the courtyard of an ancient Cambodian temple. Sod rolls out seeking shade. Observe the movie screen stretched between two sycamores and the small careful realms each scene portrays, dissolves, reconfigures. You may tire of watching or become distracted. If a scene lacks human presence, you take yourself more broadly into account. "Person possible brighten transform," says a sutra monumentalized in obsidian. "The person is possible only if brightened by transformation" is the clumsiest of interpretations. It means that you have to like this sort of thing—a world with potential and not necessarily a lot to go on. In other eras, more was spelled out. You went into the family business and fed everyone who had your last name. I know I'm oversimplifying history to promote a better future, but for now, this is our job.

Lofty Patois

After a good dinner with some physicists, we embark for the equator in one of the world's only completely wooden trucks. The streets are rife with spectators. They have assembled at curbside, parasols in hand, to witness our feat. We have memorized the contents of ancient tablets and are declaiming these antediluvian epics through loudspeakers mounted atop our vehicle. No one here has heard the indigenous language of Babylon spoken before. Upon crossing the international dateline we switch to an only recently recovered Assyrian dialect. The allure of these exotic tongues is their capacity to hold history in a state of suspended animation. Like the chug of an 1880s locomotive or the creak of a Spanish galleon, sounds of an age communicate complexities that will never be explained. You have always encouraged my intimacy with the past, but the outpouring affection and appreciation from these crowds of onlookers moves me beyond anything I'd ever hoped for.

Spokes-model

When I think of how many loads I've carried during our travels, I need a hot bath. I sink into suds and water, and the world gets all wavy. Memories of heroic leaps and stubborn hauls float away on the steam. Is this what I've been waiting for? My long-due reward? Here, with the oils and rosewater swirling in suds, I can reflect on glorious labors. Wasn't it a terrific well we sunk in the backyard? And how 'bout that insurrection we organized against the dunderheaded imperialists? As I continue to bathe, many literatures pertaining to the Bharata Natyam come to mind. Mostly they are in Sanskrit—these descriptions of Lord Nataraja's masterful dance. I have never seen or done it, but even in my exhausted fully soaked state I know I could prance, sway, and flitter for hours, becoming the ultimate exponent of this vibrant ancient art.

Croon

Some are reading and some are sunning and some study 2+2
We like the large and airy suites in our hotel's adjoining rooms
The auto-busses and oxen-drawn plows
The horizon of straw-thatched roofs

We're in a land of singing, with over a million distinguishable folk tunes. The capital is remarkable for the hefty wild rabbits running the streets and the edible mushrooms that sprout on any shaded plot of land. In our honor, the local sign painter has inscribed a special sutra on the courtyard wall facing our room. Its six characters are "electric stove," "bosom," "intrigue," "quadroon," "burro" and "replenishment." Wisdom is imparted daily as we discuss their significance. In the meantime, we've been diving off our balcony into 85° seas that roil deliciously in a lava-rock cove. Look what a wonderful arch you're getting in your descent! Miraculous as it may seem, we are all business here. You have no idea how much we've already improved relations.

Waves of Wonder

Some say that bats in flight over a moonlit mosque is a peak experience, while for us steam rising from old industrial machinery is the main treat. Of course there's the presidential palace at mid-day, when no one is around for the extensive insect humming. For many years, I meant to ask our parents about the general prognosis for pleasure and surprise, but there never seemed to be a convenient time. Social upheaval was another thing we never got around to. Will it ever be that an anarchist joins us for boat outings on a willow-draped stream? Could there be a clarity resembling revolution at heart—a fullness without narrowed conscious intention? Here's what I mean—something one could look back on and say, "How did I ever do that? I mean, what were we thinking?"

Dingy Armada

Evening tide approaches its crest. Launches increase. We are on reddening waters with our countrymen, all going to greet the battleship Potemkin on its tour of the South Seas. Are we crazy, heading our sailboat and dingy armada in the direction of those great long guns? No, this is a well-choreographed peace mission. With camera crews shooting photos from all directions, the war afoot is one of images. First prize in the local picture competition is an all-expense-paid train trip to the Black Forest, where the lucky travelers will be presented with the one and only original recipe for that region's legendary chocolate cake. For a village-bound local, this is the equivalent of a ride to Jupiter, as no one, even in their wildest dreams, considers leaving this place. Could the sex be greater elsewhere? Is there a climate anywhere that can produce such exquisite tropical woods for fetish sculpture? We've been playing up this contest, because we're inveterate continent-hoppers. Truthfully, we'd be satisfied to remain here in paradise, providing there was the occasional visitation of massive capitalist-period artifacts to remind us how good we have it and how sublime this all is.

Close Caption

It is most wonderful to look at everything as if you're about to write a letter home. There's a great wall or medieval barricade to be described in almost any old city. Foliage or the lack of it frames practically any view. Over and over again I tell the time on monumental public clocks. Any local river or standing water provides unique opportunities for reflection.

Away is what we are. Far and away. Together in bed at night we are there and dreaming. Now I'm there in thought. When you remain on shore as I float away in a catamaran, I imagine return even as I shove off.

Date palms. Denuded willow fronds. The appellation one-by-one of immense stone carbuncles. This is depth; that is undistinguished distance. When I rhapsodize the differences around me now, it is only to insure that later we are essentially the same.

Connection Charges

I am relieved. We found a cellular phone company that will let us call home. Our return will be more gradual this way—answering inane questions now instead of when we get there. "What? Of course the day gets shadowy here! Why do you think I keep looking out the window?" It makes us feel "home-bound" to talk to friends and family members stuck in their old routines. But we have a lot to share, and, quite frankly, who else cares about us enough to listen?

Did I mention that the longest dam in the world makes its river flow sideways and evaporate? That's only one of the marvels in the World's Most Modern Place. There are rice paddies with underwater lighting. The entire countryside is illuminated at night by gleaming wet terraces. And it all runs on a single AA-size rechargeable battery. Giant gulls! Colossal egg-shaped television monitors in the palm groves! Why would you ever want to leave a place like this? Actually, our behaviors are too awkward for the local inhabitants. We perform customs they swore off decades ago. We can spend only so much time feeling like rubes, though, before we want to go back to where people are less "advanced" but nicer. Still, it's hard to leave these impeccably formed sea vegetable hors d'oeuvres.

Feet First

As the world grows old we see it as dancers. *Swing Time*! It isn't the tropical climate that has aged—it's *us*. We do the cha-cha with bigger butts and look deeper into each other's eyes. Starry global night is transient, but the details of this or any evening evolve in our thoughts and intimacies. I no longer long for you, though you are scarcely in my possession. Your hand in mine, your arm around me. We have both shaved for the occasion—but on different parts of our bodies. Denuded skin can be pressed more comfortably; and we glide on, imbuing our voluptuous forms with dreams of a revolutionary universe.

Isolated Bourgeoisie

I am isolated bourgeoisie
who would gladly write for the masses
if only I knew them as friends and co-workers.
We'd talk about our families and then make plans
to renovate the world that's crushed us for generations,
knowing it has done so not as some personal vendetta,
but like unconscious machinery of misguided
motivations, interests, and lack of self-esteem.
The day is cold. The sky is blue and cloud-strewn,
my wife is recovering from alcoholism, and
we're going to Washington to protest even one more
cent being allocated for stupid B-1 bombers instead of schools.
Would you like to come? I know there's room on the
yellow bus we're borrowing from the neighborhood
vehicle cooperative. Why yes I would, but first I have to
drop by with some food for a friend on 6th Street who's
been out of work since she unionized her shop. OK,
I'll walk there with you. No let's skip. We'll get there faster.
You call this a plan? I call it action,
so far the action of writing a scenario for
social life with fewer gaps for entertainment of
privileged sentiments. A more flamboyant art will follow
on the heels of higher expectation that you will understand
in the broadest and most practical terms. The smell of toast.
Scrambling of eggs. A thorough shimmering in the
rooftop ponds. This, what is coming upon us, we are
bringing on full bore instead of suffering what we wish
were merely otherwise.

Song of the Open

Gray blowing the outside harder
gusts of fall. Small brown leaves scatter
on the supermarket roof. Even drafts
are colder, more persistent than yesterday.
The heavy whooping sound-blusters engage
the entire world in resistance and shivering.
Bernadette, the other night at St. Vincent's,
her arms palsied—she mouthed words silently
and occasionally made sense. With great confidence
she lifted the rubber penguin from the food tray to her lips
and tried to drink from its head. Sometimes
what seems to be exactly the right response
is just as surely off the mark—a routine not precise enough
to function as thought. And what makes us so smart
can barely be told or known. "The Song of the Open Road,"
all roads, all journeys, all beginnings, the spirit of invitation
to vistas beyond vistas and struggles that await discovery.
I'm singing, here, the body electric, I suppose—the compensatory
routings of brain activities from the damaged cerebellum through
other circuitry, past memory, speech and instinct.
Peggy was saying that Bernadette was most herself when
Max, Marie, and Sophie were around. Was she rising to a maternal occasion
or were there more memories to go on, more recorded response
and welcome—her mind coming most alive among the intimate and familial.
I'm supposing and romanticizing the plight of a friend the way I never
thought or wanted to see her—with faculties seemingly at bay. The power
of love and necessity of touch. The last of the ailanthus leaves
ride currents in multiple directions before dropping.

Chapter

The idea of a chapter is perfect. An episode attains completion but doesn't constitute a self-sufficient entirety. Are days and months like this? Chapters are rarely a minute. At my desk, the pretzels I was eating are gone, and the tea is just beginning. My father is still dead, and Lori is reading *Women of Wonder*, a book of science fiction stories I gave her for Christmas. If you could be here and look outside, you'd see glamorous New York City after 10.7 inches of snowfall. What an incredibly clean sky. We could complain together about capitalism and the chain of Rite Aid drugstores that infests our neighborhood. Do you empathize with the plight of independent pharmacies and bookstores? The chapter eludes me.

So listen to this! A baby car is left in the woods to find its way home. This is a rite of passage in the Chevrolet Clan. Detroit is not far away, though to an infant Chevy Malibu this distance is all the world's mileage there is. Our roadster's first task is to attract an operator—to shine and look so available that a being will climb in and drive away. The key, of course, has been left in the ignition. The smell of new gloves emanates from the upholstery. Among people, there are our desires and theirs. We possess a humanity that's to be counted on, but it's entirely beyond control.

"We are all like this baby Malibu!"

Who said that? We are not. Oh no! Are we the ones who abandoned the little auto in the first place?

I love Lori. Together we cooked all our food this week and watched the *X Files* and *Homicide: Life on the Street* instead of marching in Alabama with Martin Luther King Jr.'s Jr. Mere-ness and randomness, a lack of good homes, the fraying of our social fabric, and the wiles of unharnessed nature all protrude. What banality and haphazardness! Will loss come to dominate what has been a variously beneficial habitat? And what about this purposeful unraveling of the otherwise companionable?

Protracted War

Alluring Harbor

acrid, smoky

"Go back Señor, it's a plot!"

Ethel Merman & Bill Haywood

Ripcords.

Green tile roofs.

Pinioned.

wax impressions

attired for writhing

Chatty Sidekicks

...of Jewish cowboy fame.

Marsden Hartley & Herbie Nichols

sculptured wool carpet

By Palanquin to Antigua

sago palms

slip covers

Extortionate.

muffled reports

shivery relief

Sky According to Desire

Stallions with the Same Rash

Openly avow that thrilling dialectic.

Peachy Brocade & the Decorators

squid ink on toast

"The reefs!! We're headed for the..."

heliotrope-scented paths

Cloak the banal in dignity.

Diffusion Cold Chambers

Mine the causeway.

Nacreous Stadium Light

Clovered Landing Strips

Floodplains. Streamsides. Sandbars.

stretch in mauve flatness

Our Matador, Wilhelm

tinted glassite vials

"Labyrinthine goat pastures, Earthling!"

T*h*e F*i*s*s*u*r*e L*o*u*n*g*e

Mass work everyday.

Soothing Caveats

Rudolf Nureyev & Howlin' Wolf

all over me in cheap suits

Undraped & Palpitant

hardtop convertibles

Stymie algal bloom.

Dinah Shore

Trout Lilies & Orange Milkweed

REMOTE GLADES

Exude coziness.

"Pliant to a fault, I'd say."

wheezing wet gurgles

Moated Entranceways

yoked to a single water buffalo

All speed is made.

Flexing what's left?

Ointment Follies

The Nickel-Iron Cycle

Yenan Forum

FORMIDABLE ODDS

Cleverly bred to look like...

wiggling dampness

"Take this bozo out and ..."

Tubers. Aubergines.

maiaskin breech clouts

Make their *prahus* fast to ours.

Sensuous Young Fatties

from parts unknown

Buzz for help's promise.

Gorilla Monsoon vs. The Iron Menace

wily pumps

Impede the frump factor.

Arcuate Shorelines & Bird-foot Deltas

skittle through flesh

Avalanche Lumbago

Burgeoning Subdivisions

Rock-Waste Beaches & the Honeyed Buttes

Silty & Turbid

Coat the roof of my mouth.

Maggot. Worm. Apple grub.

jointed girder arms

Healthy Grottos

Closer to its magnetic coma...

Anaerobic Sportswomen

Bulldog Surveillance

"Why, if it isn't Uncle Lucy!"

magnesium funerary urns

Protein, the Happy Nutrient

slopes of full gown

Dainty Folds

Enchanted Stablemates

Listing Yachts

Ollie Matson, Modern Fullback

vestibules, minarets, and bracing

Oppose this feral profit arrangement!

fathomless, porcelain

fronded canal trees

clouded vistas

Run the spectrum of damson.

whole dynasties of soreheads

melt what accumulates

Sturdier. Refreshing. Enchromed.

Mr. Scrotum Takes a Holiday

Rubbery Misfits

soak our friends

"Tunics of woven lichen fiber. Nice."

somber, frigid, contradictory

Silver-leaf Scurf Peas

sprinting for intercept

Elaborate Powders

Hubby's Fiendish Intents

pulse and murmur

Truant Officers

Savor erosional remnants.

Auras on!

"Ugh, another convulsive effort."

Blanche DuBois & Billie Jean King

split and mash manioc

Heaving Blue Sea

Powwows in the Papaws

Papaws in the Powwows

portulacas *en masse*

Patrician Hussies

Zhou Enlai & Mary Lou Williams

"...tremulous, persuasive."

Starboard Radials

pleated cummerbunds

Tigerish Pajamaed Bodies

Duplicitous Mavens

swart, furtive, untidy little guys

Reflect & Ameliorate

blossoming rattlesnake root

Rampage of the Unguents

Detect & Optimize

Renegade Permission

Cowpaths to Glory

Rupture our snappy customs.

in the *tonneau*, two more blondes

fluttering warmth, the target

Remorseless Directing Mind

incognito, sort of

Diana Ross & the Supremes

winged, processional

Bywords of Loveliness

describe Beatniks

Neoteric Oaths

Katabatic Winds

You and your weenie wars

Lamentations Until Sunset

It's happy hour!

divulging everywhere!

Satchel Paige & Twiggy

Fun! Fashionable! Fantastic! Futuristic!

Grassy Blue Swales

Fire Flags & Cinnamon Ferns

If he's looking, you're showing.

tongue depressors

opened tropical night jackets

Fortunes at Will

Me? Comprador?

Basque Harpooners

Morbid. Crude. Toasty.

Tailism vs. Adventurism

Insipid Farinaceous Gruels

perceptible though not calculable

automatic but not onerous

Dilated Pupils

Dilapidated States

Glassed-in Florida Rooms

.38-caliber tracers

paddy-hulling rice mills

Labor Heroes on Ice

The Dream of Irresponsibility

seal-like, flipper-limbed

Mr. Inside & Mr. Outside

capable of penetrating any obscurity

Sow dissension & make trouble.

Hippos Grazing on Sedge

Abalone Shell Ashtrays

strangling prestige

Gapers show up gaping.

Pancho Gonzales & The Dalai Lama

Yosano Akiko & Crazy Legs Hirsch

Accruing Fertilizer

Little Ingots

Season the captor's folly.

"Listen, Gorgeous ..."

Lean-tos & Sinkholes

tungsten deposits

By Hydrofoil to Damascus

Convince me with your lips.

toadflax, deodar forest

Hal the Talking Silo

caterpillar grease

70

I waltzed with Jacqueline Onassis.

That was no tweak!

Take a tip from the Tunisians.

Dihedral Soaring

shallow slab-lined pits for homes

Stain the lips pastelessly.

Roseate Sandstone & the Dimpled Escarpments

Retard the end run.

owns it—hones it—tones it

buoyed by the kelp forest

Primp for surgery.

swarming with sampans

Slough along in bunny slippers.

Queer it with bluing.

Redwood Sun Decks

Erratic Troths

Spell E-L-D-O-R-A-D-O in misty gold letters.

Jimmy Durante & Cecil B. DeMille

Wave languidly.

agitation provoked by lack

agitation provoked by glut

Emblemize at nightmare velocity.

fluffy delphinium-blue feathers

doused with the perfume Quarry

Creamy Hemispheres

Barbados cherry hedges

silhouetted, low-scudding

A Salt Lick for Uncle Arnoldo

bruised shapeless

my massive, oily length

That's no limp! It's a sashay!

Oolite

Oranges. Biscuits. Water-lilies.

Elucidate fiascoes.

"My eye on myself was fascinated."

Garbo radiant against the snow

trouble up front

creases sewn in

trouble down below

Voracious Snoopers

Lingering Night Mists

panne, velvet, hammered satin

72

The Tidal Bore of the Revolution

assiduously wooed

Dolorous Spell & the Nods

Rise to mating status.

Fluid. Fleeting. Borderless.

homespun soaked with resin

Feudal Land Rents

Serve a spurious unity.

The Eye's Unfailing Logic

truncated summits

Possessive Case

Throttles Jerked Wide

"Now, I merely jiggle the ailerons & ..."

white espaliered lantana

mimosa, olive, orange & lemon

mired in victory-seeking.

Mastabahs of Chufu

Hotbeds of Cadre Activity

Him not walk as ordinary boy.

Her not walk like ordinary girl.

Kim Basinger in *Macbeth*

flaming tongues, a legume?

73

contours beneath the torn underthings

My Turbine Superstructure

zoom! Zoom!! ZOOM!!!

Free

Fall through the world. Improvement after improvement. T-shirts
swing in air, wolf hoots, corn cob squadrons fly in formation, folded
blue rice cookies, lime-green fortune papers inside, polished basalt
monuments, vinyl coves, a nation of wet undergarments, vanilla,
remote control volcanoes, chrome dice, blanched pickles, live mink
on tour, ornate racing flags, occasional nails, clay fedoras, principled
neighbors, lath, cinnamon, crosshatches. Forget dichondra lawns,
absolute cherry petals, crocus, and blooming magnolia. The painted
trellis whose bottle green rubs off as powder when touched, the
pigment, I mean, green door, brass fittings.

2

Home away edges an archipelago beyond the supermarket. Let's pre-
meditate not only but to never on the side. Your presentation of an
embankment follows merchandise. From me chrysanthemums are
originally panic. Practice thrift in a barn. Wiggly things. Brittle slate
bars. All knocked around to ventilate our companion hydrofoil. Your
games to my sediment. Lofty buns. Corrugated in the drive-bys.
Pleasure those Cub Scouts, oh rolly ones.

3

Folly narrows, wild and penetrating. A whiff of tuned gray matter.
Elms, the forgiven ones. Wrists and dress the brood-width declines. Is
there a foreign to life the sanction way. Meet the fig layer. Prove in
melody all that leafs. Sand winds for botany sedge the cuffs of lamb
and whey. Dubbed and clingy. Wad and prey. Falls the east, no quid
magnificent. Barley flung, gone potting day.

4

Saturation at the helm. Four locks. Deep in the biting is a customizer, prudent and wickerless. Dimes in a dime store. Protein is a mouthful. We are absolutely amazed that combustibles hold our future of heat and light. We magnify dove warnings to any bank of livery bums. Principals have gold hickory nuts? We preside and alleviate hailstorms. Ooh goody, a song or diorama about the coming of mercurochrome. My what a stain and phosphor. Orange with floaters is inside my eyes.

5

All you know of me is capacity. The capture of Pago Pago by lighting designers. Frothed up and stashed away, this morning you might hunt for lost socks and find a persimmon. Styling regret as the freest temptation to laminate glossy holdings. Plinths knock knees. Doleful primpings. Discern our flagrant saga. This spiraled analysis outshone the Hegelians. You fathom and fathom in lyric and melody. Propel what is instantly laden. This is splendid meadow. Strewn peacock feathers direct our meanderings. What necessitates trust is the guided and free.

6

Look at this, perceptions are missed. Damp air. Green casts a coat over the floorboards and walls, and my skin slants protected. Angels fly up but who are they? Empty of will, we comfort the state. It is impregnable. Stone walls topped by electrified barb wire. Dirt beneath the barrier is mined with poison gas. How will we prevail or come to terms with the mightiness of evil? Don't think of it that way; it will only hurt you.

7

On the salts, rude as paste to fawn over, we slip down, prolific as day. Menace the fine patients. In the patrol of bird sanctuaries, winter fowl consider themselves lucky: melted ice to float on, food to dive for. What fat under the skin is so watertight and heat-proof? Am I Thoreau? No. I don't make a big deal of glory and trying to reduplicate. Nope nope nope. Riggings on the pant-legs of our pursuer. Snow rows and sky planes. We press on, and a wind blows up gauged against oak trunks. Breathe and scan. A future of futures awaits us, novel and sublime.

8

It was a sunny afternoon, and I was being quite free with my multiplication tables. 4 x 4. 8 x 3. No one was responding as I'd hoped but I continued to challenge my family with numeric wizardry. Now subtract the numerological value of your license plate from our street number and divide it by the combined E.R.A. of the Brooklyn Dodgers' pitchers in 1955. It was a World Series year, 1955, but I knew nothing about it at the time.

By 6 p.m., clouds enveloped our neighborhood in pre-dusk gloom. Rain began to fall and I could smell a meal cooking several rooms away. Mom, who was cooking, was my mother, and we'd been together as much as possible for a good number of years by then.

Next, I'm going to recount the tale of a mole who wished she was an Indonesian flying fish. There aren't a lot of details, but in essence the yens of a tunneling rodent are vivid once we tune them in. Darkness in the burrowed world is varied, but to be of blue sky over trembling water and remain aloft until our scales dry has riveting appeal.

9

Instant fresh tables divide and drop leaves. Far and away I'm a frontier. You scuffle around and squeak the floor boards. Motors outside and coal shovels crunch. Enter a nude parking lot. Odors of steam and cleaning solvents. We'll stay in the car all day and rub our slick upholstery; fashion soft amber light or something porous and fragrant. Times being what they are, thought flows upward. Red turtleneck smocks. See, religion is easy. Fooled trees implicate a bomber's whereabouts. How I'm ringing it by you. Precious, genteel: this permeable implosion of street life, curbs, my morning's wild splendor. What we embrace recalls Buick sedans, leaning against sweat, pleased to be stabile in such fine condition.

10

Saharan heat waves. Lawrence of Arabia, Englishman in Bedouin garb, achieves an identity that wasn't possible at home, where he'd have had it in mind to be someone else, but nobody could let him. Imagine cucumbers in a frosty salad. Is that you? Of course it is. Seek prime directives that last only as long as they're interesting. Marvelous, these floral globules are savory shadows leading on and on. Stables and the smell of horse shit and hay camouflage our damp thicket hideout. Travel, edging through, is struggle and release.

11

Here where you might wind up deep blue night, we've entered as pinkies riding formulaic leaves. We find a good gait with plenary molting. Finally the haven of basic propulsion, we reach formal sleep. Clouds gather into even blackness. Why not animals priming coral panes? They're poses. If only I still had young skin.

12

Feel that notch with your thumb? When you do, stop. Now, go over to the window and make sure the hose is inside the garbage can. Let's take a break: five luscious bulges from the natural and unnatural worlds, followed by three moist insertions. Somebody recites a summer seed catalogue. Next, a woman says, "It's all political. You can't say this is love and that's political. What if farmers did that?" A man from the next room: "You know I can take a hard line too. I'm sick of your sister-in-law acting as if I'm ruining plans. I know what a vocation is." Are these two intimate? What if he's a carpenter and she's the interior designer for a local housing project?

13

Story is inevitable because I'm not singing or extolling your virtues. I'm a-tremble with fortune. Gads. Everything. We roll on and nothing cups up to the one-trick pony. Horn honks. A plaid-uniformed student crosses the perfectly paved street on a cool morning. Can a yellow bus ever be as exciting as freesia? My emblem is struck on Indian manhole covers. I can't picture whole boatloads of them floating across the sea. Anything called sex after the revolution is a movie.

14

Down a thin ramp we roll in miniature ant-baby carriages. Dunes spread to the purple horizon. You see stars and planets before a monoprop mail plane putters across the sky humming. Try delirious dog-barks, while I disguise the insignia of our foremothers with felt-tip pen and gold leaf. Mark this capillary for rude promises. How is it we crackle when smooth slurping falls to gardeners only half our size? Problems ensue.

15

Dream life is wholesome. The phony R sign on the filling station doesn't mean ReveRse. It signifies Revel so we immediately do, by buRsting into song and gaRment exchanges. I'm weaRing Ralph's T-shiRt and Robin's pants. Rudy has my tie aRound his head as a haiR band. R customized engine suppoRts RevolutionaRy acts in all countRies undeR colonial Rule oR impeRialist sway. "TomoRRow" has the same meaning as when we weRe fiRst dRiving, but it doesn't come up a lot. "What's next, a Rodeo?" If you don't caRe to mount a BRahma bull the fiRst time out, lick its hoRns, make fRiends, take tuRns as staR and staRlet. Ensemble woRk is too plangent foR R.e.m. sleep. DReam and life Roll on in R lithe fRames.

16

In dreams air is immaculate moisture that cleans and lubricates. Purify desire leave ready for more. Appointment after appointment. In perpetual arousal morning promises. The size of rips unmeasured, begin fastening. Imagine public stories bear on private life. Arson kills five. If you never take a commuter train to Washington DC, you wouldn't have been on the one crushed yesterday by an Amtrak freighter that was on the same tracks. Resolve not to ride in the first car, because everyone in there was killed, and if it's your world the TV is reporting on, you have reason to believe similar catastrophes will occur again. A disaster is like the sunrise that way. A new period begins in which a possibility has made itself evident. Fine. I can live with that. Make understudies stand tall. Assign red on carpets every excellent day.

17

Start from zero, one blink past the pigeons and the sky openings to steady floaters downstream where candles lift from waves to light ripples. I am lamb boy. All the groves and none of the hubcaps roll without flinches. Force inquiries. There's fuel because you mine coal fields and stretch cabling. Brick towers interrupting our horizon views impel the invasion of clean spirits. Isn't it simply intoxicating to be called "oh great one." Let's go on this way until you get tired.

What we know about specifics is that they're a whole story unto themselves. I'm in a car seat but it's not attached to a vehicle, unless you consider a planet or continent your steed. I don't but the immensity of the birds around here makes me nervous. They sidle up to tourists and peck. Peck peck peck. Pretty soon I've dropped everything and I'm laughing hysterically, "Oh, you big pecker you, ha ha ha, cut it out."

18

Flatten trilling and plow under the bed-linen departments. Timings go pale. I am blackstrap molasses then fond lining odors. Angular green alphabets. No alternative prairie postings intimate not grappling. Wax builds up on the carelessly shiny, and brick by brick a monumental human takes hold. I know all about spousal pride. Mickey lifts the clothes iron over his head and mumbles, "Anyone want a flat top?" Can you blame Minnie for grabbing her car keys and running out the door? A puzzled mouse face incites laughter, but when Mickey takes the toaster for a walk, we know we're in for a long afternoon. I like it best when fluffy houses and trees waver in the animated background to strains of hot Parisian jazz. Sidney Bechet. What would he do to someone who is totally inept? Anxious to forgive all, we strike out and attain.